AF435238

Teach Your Children

The Essential Knowledge

of

Islam

OMER SULAYMAN

Copyright 2022

In the Name of Allah,
The Most Merciful,
The Bestower of Mercy!

Table of Contents

LESSON 01

WHAT EVERY CHILD SHOULD KNOW

Question: Who is your Lord?

Answer: My Lord is Allah!

Question: What is your Religion?

Answer: My Religion is Islam!

Question: Who is your Prophet?

Answer: My Prophet is Muhammad (peace and blessings of Allah be upon him)

Ask your child to fill in the gaps with the appropriate words:

My Lord is..........

My Religion is..........

My Prophet is..........

Make your child to memorize these words of remembrance of Allah to be said every morning and evening (three times) along with their meaning:

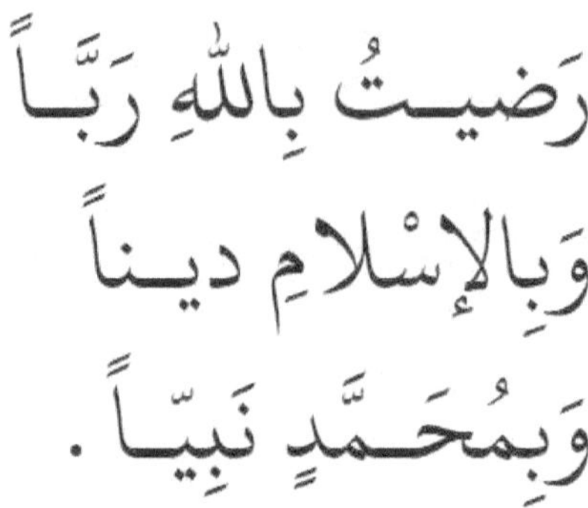

"Raḍītu billāhi Rabba, wa bil-Islāmi dīna, wa bi-Muḥammadin (ṣallallāhu ʿalayhi wa sallama) nabiyya." (I am pleased with Allah as my Lord, with Islam as my religion and with Muhammad (peace and blessings of Allah be upon him) as my Prophet!

NOTES TO THE PARENT AND TEACHER:

Explain to your child the superiority of Allah Almighty over His Creation such as humans, because He created the people from nothing and endowed them with blessings that they use to worship only Him alone.

Tell him or her about the mercy of Allah to His servants, because He sent to them a Messenger, whose name was Muhammad, peace and blessings of Allah be upon him. The one who obeys the Prophet, peace and blessings of Allah be upon him, will have success and happiness in this world and in life after death (the Hereafter).

Explain to the child the greatness of the Islamic religion, which Allah has blessed His servants with. For Allah Almighty has said:

"This day I have perfected for you your religion and completed My favor upon you and have approved for you Islam as religion" (Surah al-Maidah, verse 3).

Plant the seeds of reverence for Islam in the souls of your children.

Purpose of this lesson:

To explain to the child what each person should know. To inspire the child with love and respect for the Islamic religion.

Teach your child that after mentioning the name of the Prophet, one should say a prayer for him, saying in Arabic: "Salla - Allahu alayhi wa sallam", which is translated as, "Peace be upon him and the blessings of Allah!" It is obligatory for every Muslim when mentioning the Messenger of Allah (peace and blessings of Allah be upon him) to say these words. Allah says: "Indeed, Allah confers blessing upon the Prophet, and His angels [ask Him to do so]. O you who have believed, ask [Allah to confer] blessing upon him and ask [Allah to grant him] peace." (al - Ahzab 33:56).

LESSON 02

MY LORD ALLAH

Question: Who is your Lord?

Answer: My Lord is Allah.

Question: Where is Allah?

Answer: Allah is above the heavens (skies)

Question: Who created you and raised you with His Mercy?

Answer: Allah created me and raised me with His graces!

NOTES TO THE PARENT AND TEACHER:

Sharia evidence of the presence of Allah above the heavens is a hadith, which tells about a girl - a slave, who, to the question of the Messenger of Allah: "Where is Allah?", (she) answered: **"(Allah is) Above the heavens"** (Sahih Muslim, No. 5308).

Explain to the child the meaning of the expression: "Allah raised me with His graces." It means: "Allah has strengthened me with external and internal favors. Outer favors include safety, health, and well-being. The inner graces include faith (*iman*) and guidance on the true path (***hidaya***). Place the greatness of Allah in the soul of the child.

Purpose of this lesson:

1- Arouse in the children the desire to exalt Allah Almighty.

2- Explain to the children that Allah is above His creations.

3- Remind the children of some of Allah's favors on His creations.

LESSON 03

KNOWING ABOUT THE LORD

I come to know my Lord through His signs and through His creatures, such as night, day, heaven and earth.

Allah gave me life, then He will give me death, and to Him is the return.

TOPIC FOR DISCUSSION

Ask your child: How do you know about your Lord?

Question (Ask him or her): Who gave you life and then will give you death?

NOTES TO THE PARENT AND TEACHER:

Mention to the child the other actions of Allah Almighty! For example, sending down rain, growing plants, answering his or her prayers, getting rid of his or her sorrows and hardships.

Encourage the children to contemplate on the signs of Allah and His creations.

Explain the meaning of the word the 'return (*nushur*) to Allah'. It means resurrection after death to report on their deeds and recompense for them. Place faith in the resurrection after death in the souls of the children.

Purpose of this lesson:

Remind the children of some of the signs of Allah and His creations.

Encourage the children to contemplate on the signs of Allah and His creations.

Explain to the children that Allah Almighty will resurrect people after their death to account for their deeds and retribution.

LESSON 04

ALLAH IS THE CREATOR (al-Khaliq)

Allah created me and all people.

Allah created the heavens and the earth.

Allah created night and day, sun and moon.

Fill in the gaps with the appropriate words:

.... created all creations.

..................created the heavens and the earth.

.... created the sun and the moon.

NOTES TO THE PARENT AND TEACHER:

Explain to the children that the greatness of creation indicates the greatness of their Creator, therefore only Allah deserves to be worshiped.

Try to get the children to think about the greatness of creations of Allah, such as the sky, earth and trees.

Together with your the children, give other examples of the creations of Allah Almighty.

Encourage the children to contemplate on the creations of Allah so that they feel the greatness of Allah Almighty who created them.

Purpose of this lesson:

Encourage the children to contemplate on the creations of Allah Almighty in order to inspire them with a sense of His greatness.

Explain to the children the mercy of Allah Almighty to people, because He created them from nothing.

ALLAH IS THE CREATOR

Allah created the mountains, seas and trees.

Allah Almighty said: "Allah is the Creator of all things, and He is, over all things, Disposer of affairs." (Surah az-Zumar, ayat 62).

Therefore, I am obliged to worship only Allah alone, Who created everything.

TOPIC FOR DISCUSSION

List the above three things that Allah has created!

Allah is the Creator of all things. Bring Sharia evidence (proof from the Quran or Hadith) for these words!

Allah Almighty said: "He is the One Who gave the sun radiance and the moon light." (Surah Yunus, verse 5).

NOTES TO THE PARENT AND TEACHER:

Explain to the children that Allah alone is the only Creator. Explain to the children that only He alone needs to be worshiped.

Allah is the Creator of all things.

Mention to the children the benefits of certain creatures, such as the seas and trees.

Purpose of this lesson:

Remind the children of some of Allah's creations.

Remind the children of the *reference from the Quran or Authentic Hadeeth* that Allah is the Creator of all things (Quote to them a verse from the Quran such as the one mentioned above which proves that Allah is the Creator of all things).

Encourage the children to contemplate on the creations of Allah.

LESSON 05

SOME MIRACLES OF THE POWER OF ALLAH, MANIFESTED IN HIS CREATIONS

"Our Lord! You didn't create this aimlessly. You are pure (exalted above such a thing)! Protect us from the torment of the Fire!" (Surah Aali 'Imran, ayat 191).

It's amazing how one can disobey Allah, and how an unbeliever dares to deny that He exists, when there is His sign in everything, which indicates that He is the only One who is worthy of Worship.

Only the Creator of all things deserves to be worshipped!

NOTES TO THE PARENT AND TEACHER:

Explain to the children the different aspects of the greatness of the creations of Allah, so that they can realize it.

Explain to the children that contemplating on the signs of Allah increases the faith of a Muslim, knowledge of His Lord, love for Him and reverence for Him. It is necessary that you encourage the children to reflect on the creations of Allah Almighty that surround them, while explaining the benefits that these creations bring to man and other creatures.

Purpose of this lesson:

Explain to the children the different aspects of the greatness of the creations of Allah.

Encourage the children to contemplate on the signs of Allah and His creations.

LESSON 06

ALLAH IS THE PROVIDER

Allah sends down rain from the sky.

Allah gives us food and drink.

Allah gave us hearing and sight.

TOPIC FOR DISCUSSION

Question (Ask the child): Who gave us food and drink?

Complete the following sentences:

1- I use my sight through the Mercy of.............

2- I use my hearing through the Mercy of............

NOTES TO THE PARENT AND TEACHER:

Tell the children about the benefits of rain.

Emphasize to the children that it is necessary to conserve water and not to waste it. Also one must not waste food.

Develop in the child gratitude for the favors of Allah since this is the reason for their increase, because the Almighty Allah said: "If you are grateful, then I will give you even more" (Surah Ibrahim, ayat 7).

Point out to the children the great benefits that hearing and sight bring.

Tell that that Allah has endowed us with great mercies, which include food, drink, hearing and sight, so that through this we have the strength to obey Him.

Purpose of this lesson:

Remind the children of some of the mercies of Allah. Encourage the children to thank Allah for His favors.

ALLAH IS THE PROVIDER (*ar-Razzaq* – the Bestower of Sustenance)

Allah gave us health and safety

Allah Almighty has said: "Indeed, Allah is the Sustainer, the Mighty, the Strong." (Surah al-Dhariyat, verse 58).

Therefore, I must thank Allah, Who has endowed me with everything!

TOPIC FOR DISCUSSION

Question: Who gave us everything?

Complete the following sentence:

A Muslim thanks his Lord for every mercy shown and says: "...............................!" (Al-hamdu li-llah! – Praise be to Allah)

What will be the state of the earth if Allah does not rain on it? (...)

What will be the state of the earth when Allah sends rains on it? (...)

NOTES TO THE PARENT AND TEACHER:

Explain to the children that only Allah Almighty alone should be asked to grant us the means of subsistence.

Encourage the children to ask Allah for health and security.

Encourage the children to say, "Al - hamdu li - llah!" ("Praise be to Allah!") for every mercy.

Mention examples of other favors of Allah. The Righteous Predecessors (the companions of the Prophet, Allah be pleased with them, and the next 2 generations) said: "The mention of graces (the favors, blessings, and mercies of Allah) evokes the love of the Bestower of mercy, the Exalted and Blessed!"

Purpose of this lesson:

Remind the children of the Sharia evidence (proof from the Quran and authentic Hadith) indicating that Allah grants livelihood.

Encourage the children to thank Allah for the great favors of the Almighty.

LESSON 07

I WORSHIP ALLAH, MY LORD!

I am a Muslim. I worship only Allah.

I am a Muslim. I love Allah and obey Him.

I am a Muslim. I fear Allah and obey Him.

I am a Muslim. I pray only to Allah and do not call with prayers to anyone else along with Him.

TOPIC FOR DISCUSSION

Question: Who alone do we worship?

Fill in the gaps with the following words:

Paradise, Prayer, Quran, Allah

A Muslim prays only to..................

A Muslim strictly observes the implementation of..........

A Muslim reads a lot of.............. in order to achieve the pleasure of Allah and enter into..................

NOTES TO THE PARENT AND TEACHER:

Explain to the children that Allah is the Creator, the Giver of sustenance, the Giver of life, the Sender of death, and He alone is worthy and deserving of worship.

Mention different types of worship such as prayer, fasting, supplication, sacrifice, etc.

Encourage the children to perform acts of obedience to Allah.

Purpose of this lesson:

- Encourage the children to worship only Allah alone and no one else along with Him.

- Remind the children of certain types of worship.

- To evoke in the children a sense of pride in the Islamic religion.

LESSON 08

MY RELIGION IS ISLAM!

I am a Muslim. My religion is Islam

The Almighty said: "Verily, the religion of Allah is Islam." (Surah Aali 'Imran, verse 19).

Islam is:

Worshiping only Allah, obedience to Him, refusing to disobey Him, and keeping away from any religion other than Islam.

TOPIC FOR DISCUSSION

Question: What is your religion?

NOTES TO THE PARENT AND TEACHER:

Explain to the children the meaning of Islam and plant love for this great religion in the souls of the children by mentioning the distinctive features of Islam.

Explain to the children that only by firmly adhering to Islam can one enter Paradise and be saved from Hell.

Explain to the children that it is part of Islam to love Muslims and hate unbelievers (since they don't worship Allah alone), and tell them to not be like the unbelievers.

Purpose of this lesson:

Explain to the children the meaning of Islam.

To inspire the children with love for Muslims.

Warn the children against polytheism and polytheists.

MY RELIGION IS ISLAM

Allah Almighty said:

And whoever desires other than Islam as religion –
never will it be accepted from him, and he, in the
Hereafter, will be among the losers.
(Surah "Aali 'Imran", ayat 85).

Thus, I am a Muslim and do not accept any religion
other than Islam!

TOPIC FOR DISCUSSION

Question: What is the basis of Islam?

Fill in the gaps in the following sentence with the appropriate words
(Islam, Hell)

Every religion except .... is false. Whoever dies
outside of Islam will fall into ....

Allah does not accept any other religion than Islam. Give Sharia evidence for this statement (refer to the verse from the Quran above).

NOTES TO THE PARENT AND TEACHER:

When the Messenger of Allah, peace and blessings of Allah be upon him, sent Muadh, may Allah be pleased with him, to the people of Yemen, the first thing he told him to invite them (the people of Yemen) to the Testimony that - none has the right to be worshipped but Allaah and that I (the Prophet Muhammad – peace and blessings of Allah be upon him) am the Messenger of Allaah). (Bukhari 7372 and Muslim 19).

Explain to the children the greatness and importance of the two testimonies - by which a non-Muslim enters Islam is to say: ***Ashhadu an laa ilaaha illa Allaah wa anna Muhammadan Rasool Allaah***; which means that none has the right to be worshipped but Allaah and that Muhammad is the Messenger of Allaah. The first Testimony means affirming and having a firm belief that it is Allaah alone Who is worthy of worship, and the second Testimony means affirming and having a firm belief that Muhammad is truly a Messenger sent from Allaah.

Give examples of false religions – all other religions besides Islam. Explain that whoever dies outside of Islam will go to Hell.

Purpose of this lesson:

Remind the children of the basis of Islam.

Instill in the children a sense of pride in the Islamic religion.

Explain to the children that any religion other than Islam is false.

LESSON 09

MY PROPHET IS MUHAMMAD (peace and blessings of Allah be upon him!)

My Prophet is Muhammad *ibn* (son of) Abdullah *ibn* (who was the son of) Abdulmuttalib.

Allah sent him (peace and blessings of Allah be upon him) to all people.

Allah sent him to call them to the worship of Allah alone, and so that they (the people) refuse to worship anything other than Allah.

TOPIC FOR DISCUSSION

Fill in the gaps with the appropriate words:

The Prophet's name is
....

Allah sent him to ....

Allah sent him to call them to ....

NOTES TO THE PARENT AND TEACHER:

One of the favors of Allah to His servants is that He sent the Prophet Muhammad (peace and blessings of

Allah be upon him!) to them, who called them to worship only Allah alone.

Explain to the children that one of the requirements of love for the Messenger (peace and blessings of Allah be upon him) lies in obeying his orders and following him.

Warn against worshiping anyone other than Allah.

Encourage the invocation of blessings on the Prophet (peace and blessings of Allah be upon him!) at the mention of him.

Purpose of this lesson:

Remind the children of the genealogy of the Prophet Muhammad (peace and blessings of Allah be upon him!).

Remind the children that Allah Almighty sent Muhammad (peace and blessings of Allah be upon him!) to all people.

Explain to the children the wisdom that the Prophet Muhammad (peace and blessings of Allah be upon him!) was sent to the people.

MY PROPHET IS MUHAMMAD (peace and blessings of Allah be upon him!)

Whoever obeys the Messenger (peace and blessings of Allah be upon him!) will go to Paradise.

Whoever disobeys the Messenger (peace and blessings of Allah be upon him!) will go to Hell.

THAT'S WHY:

I must love the Messenger (peace and blessings of Allah be upon him!) and obey him.

TOPIC FOR DISCUSSION

Fill in the gaps with the appropriate words:

Whoever obeys the Messenger (peace and blessings of Allah be upon him!), will go to ....

Whoever disobeys the Messenger (peace and blessings of Allah be upon him!), will go to ....

What should be said when the name of the Messenger of Allah is mentioned?
....

NOTES TO THE PARENT AND TEACHER:

Encourage the children to obey the Messenger (peace and blessings of Allah be upon him!) and love him. Warn the against contradicting what the Prophet ordered (peace and blessings of Allah be upon him!).

Point out that the one who loves the Messenger (peace and blessings of Allah be upon him!) will be with him in Paradise, as reported in the following hadith: "A person will be with the one he loves" (Sahih al - Bukhari, No. 6169).

Mention some of the noble qualities of the Messenger (peace and blessings of Allah be upon him), for example, about his truthfulness, so that the children would love the Prophet (peace and blessings of Allah be upon him!) even more and wish to follow him.

Give examples of love and obedience to the Prophet (peace and blessings of Allah be upon him) by the Companions (may Allah be pleased with them!). Also mention that they never disobeyed him.

Purpose of this lesson:

Explain to the children that love for the Prophet (peace and blessings of Allah be upon him!) is expressed in obedience to him and by following his example.

Explain to the children that whoever obeys the Messenger (peace and blessings of Allah be upon him!) will go to Paradise, and whoever disobeys him will go to Hell.

Warn the children of the danger of contradicting what the Messenger (peace and blessings of Allah be upon him!) ordered.

LESSON 10

BLESSED QURAN

Allah Almighty sent down the Blessed Qur'an to His Messenger Muhammad (peace and blessings of Allah be upon him!).

The Blessed Qur'an is the Speech of Allah Almighty.

It is necessary to love the Qur'an, read it and act in accordance with it.

TOPIC FOR DISCUSSION

What is the name of the Book that Allah Almighty sent down to His Messenger Muhammad (peace and blessings of Allah be upon him!)? ....

Fill in the gaps with the appropriate words:

I am Muslim. My Book is the Blessed....................

Prophet Muhammad (peace and blessings of Allah be upon him!) said: "The best of you is the one who .... the Quran and teaches it (others)"

Teach the children and let them memorize the ayat of the "Throne" (ayat al - Kursi). Make them read it after every prayer and before going to bed.

NOTES TO THE PARENT AND TEACHER:

Tell the story of the beginning of the sending down of the Blessed Qur'an to the Messenger of Allah (peace and blessings of Allah be upon him!) in the cave of Hira in words suitable for the children to understand.

Plant sprouts of love for the Blessed Qur'an in the souls of the children.

Encourage the children to read the Blessed Qur'an and memorize it, keeping in mind the reward that a person receives for this is only from Allah. The Prophet (peace and blessings of Allah be upon him!) said: "The best of you is the one who studies the Quran and teaches it (to others)" ("Sahih" al - Bukhari, No. 5027). The Prophet (peace and blessings of Allah be upon him!) also said: "Whoever reads at least one letter from the Qur'an, (one) good deed will be written, and for (every) good deed (the reward is) tenfold, and I do not say that "Alif, Lam, Mim" is one letter, no, (but) "Alif" is a letter, "Lam" is a letter and "Mim" is a letter" ("Sunan" at - Tirmidhi, No. 2910).

Remind the children of the need to show respect for the Blessed Quran and to exalt it, and also to remain silent when listening to the Quran, based on the following Words of the Almighty as a proof: "When the Quran is recited, then listen to it and keep silence - perhaps you will have mercy" (Surah Al-A'raf, verse 204).

Mention other names of the Qur'an, for example, the Reminder (az - Dhikr), the Criterion (al - Furqan), the Scripture (al - Kitab).

Encourage the children to act in accordance with the Blessed Quran, by carrying out the orders contained therein and avoiding the prohibitions mentioned therein.

Purpose of this lesson:

Explain to the children that the Blessed Quran is the Speech of Allah.

Remind the children to show respect for the Blessed Quran.

Point out to the children the need to follow the orders contained in the Qur'an.

Point out to the children the need to avoid the prohibitions mentioned in the Qur'an.

LESSON 11

The three fundamentals that a person should know are

1 - The slave's knowledge of his Lord

2 - The slave's knowledge of his religion

3 - Knowledge of a slave about his Prophet (peace and blessings of Allah be upon him)

The Prophet (peace and blessings of Allaah be upon him) said: "The sweetness of faith will be felt by the one who is satisfied with Allah as his Lord, Islam as his religion and Muhammad (peace and blessings of Allaah be upon him) as his Prophet" (narrated by Muslim in his Sahih, No. 34).

TOPIC FOR DISCUSSION

Fill in the gaps with the appropriate words:

The three fundamentals that a person should know are

1   –   Knowledge   of   the   slave   about   his
....

2   –   Knowledge   of   the   slave   about   his
....

3   -   Knowledge   of   the   slave   about   his
....

What is the Sharia evidence for the three foundations that a person should know?

In his grave, the servant of Allah **will be asked three questions**:

Who is your Lord?

What is your religion?

Who is your Prophet?

NOTES TO THE PARENT AND TEACHER:

Explain to the children the word "base or foundation", meaning the main part of an object that serves as its support.

Explain to the children that the servant of Allah will be asked about these three fundamentals in his grave (Who is your Lord? What is your religion? Who is your Prophet?). Whoever answers these questions correctly, Allah will reward with the Paradise, and whoever does not answer them, Allah will subject him to a painful punishment.

Purpose of this lesson:

Tell the children about these three basic questions.

Point out to the children the reference from the Quran or Authentic Hadeeth of these three foundations.

Inspire pride and respect for the Islamic religion in the children.

LESSON 12

Three basics

- The knowledge of the slave about his Lord

- The knowledge of the slave of his religion

– Knowledge of a slave about his Prophet (peace and blessings of Allah be upon him)

My Lord is Allah who is The Creator (al - Khaliq), the Provider (ar - Razzaq).

He alone and no one else deserves to be worshipped.

I come to know my Lord through His signs and through His creation, such as the night, day, sun, moon, heaven and earth.

Allah Almighty said:

"Among His signs are the night and the day, the sun and the moon. Do not prostrate yourself before the sun and moon, but prostrate yourself before Allah, Who created them, if you worship Him."
(Surah Fussilat, verse 37).

TOPIC FOR DISCUSSION

What is the meaning of the word "Lord" (ar - Rabb)?

Fill in the gaps with the appropriate words:

I know about my Lord through His................and through His ....

The one who created night and day is ....

Emphasize the signs of Allah in the following verse:

"Do you not see that Allah lengthens the day at the expense of the night and lengthens the night at the expense of the day, and subdued the sun and the moon, which move towards the appointed time, and that Allah is aware of what you do?" (Surah Luqman, verse 29).

The sun and the moon are among the great creations of Allah, which Allah has bestowed upon us by His Grace. What are the benefits of the Sun and Moon?

I am a Muslim. I am convinced that Allah created creations and endowed them with livelihood. Allah is in charge of all the affairs of this Universe and only He alone deserves to be worshiped!

NOTES TO THE PARENT AND TEACHER:

Take the children in the street to visually show them the greatness of the creations of Allah, while referring to the relevant verses of the Qur'an and hadiths.

Allah Almighty said: "O people! Worship your Lord who created you and those before you, so that you may be afraid (of Allah). He made the earth a bed for you, and the sky a roof, He sent down water from the sky and with it brought forth fruits for your sustenance. Therefore, do not deliberately equate anyone with Allah." (Surah al - Baqarah, verses 21-22).

Ibn Kathir (Allah have mercy on him) said: "The creator of these things deserves to be worshiped."

Explain to the children that contemplating on the creations of Allah is worship.

Encourage the children to turn to Allah with supplications both in well-being (for example, that they ask Allah for beneficial knowledge and lawful livelihood, that is *halal rizq*), and in misfortune (for example, that they ask Allah to heal from illness and to relieve hardships). Encourage the children to thank Allah for His great mercies, which include the Sun and Moon in particular, because they contain great benefits for humans, animals and plants.

Purpose of this lesson:

Explain to the children the first of the three fundamentals (that is their Lord).

Explain to the children the meaning of the word "Lord" (ar - Rabb).

Enumeration by the children of some creations of Almighty Allah.

LESSON 13

Allah created jinn and humans only for them to worship Him alone!

The reference from the Quran or Authentic Hadeeth of this is the Words of Almighty Allah: "And I created jinn and people only so that they worship Me" (Surah "adh-Dhariyat", ayat 56).

Worship (al-ibadah)

This is a collective designation of everything that Allah loves and is pleased with, whether it be words or deeds, obvious or hidden.

Examples of worship:

Love for Allah, fear of Allah, prayers to Allah, prayer (*Salah*), fasting, honoring parents.

TOPIC FOR DISCUSSION

Allah created you because of great Wisdom. What is this wisdom? Give reference from the Quran or Authentic Hadeeth for this. (reference from the Quran and authentic Hadeeth)!

Fill in the gaps with the appropriate words:

Worship is a collective term for everything that Allah loves and is pleased with, whether it be .... or ...., obvious or ....

The types of worship include prayer, ..., ... ,..............

Allah Almighty said: "The believing men and women who acted righteously, We will certainly give a beautiful life and reward the best of what they did." (Surah "an - Nahl", ayat 97).

Through what is a beautiful life achieved?

Worship - the reason for opening the chest (for truth) and calming the hearts

NOTES TO THE PARENT AND TEACHER:

Explain to the children that in all the creations of Allah and in all His commands there is wisdom. In particular, man was not simply created. Rather he was created for a great cause, which is to worship only Allah alone and not to associate partners with Him. Allah Almighty said:

"Did you think we created you for uselessly?" (Surah "al - Muminun", ayat 115).

Mention other types of worship, such as external (otherwise called "deeds of the body" - for example, zakat, hajj, and sacrifice), and internal (otherwise called "deeds of the heart" - for example, love, fear, hope, etc..)

Explain that worship is the cause of the opening of the chest. Allah Almighty said: "The believing men and women who acted righteously, We will certainly give a beautiful life and reward the best of what they did." (Surah "an - Nahl", ayat 97).

Purpose of this lesson:

1- Explain to the children the wisdom in the creation of jinn and people.

2- Explain to the children the meaning of the word "worship".

3- Remind the children of the Shari'ah evidence pointing to the wisdom of the creation of jinn and humans.

LESSON 14

The greatest thing that Allah has commanded is monotheism (*tawhid*).

Monotheism is the worship of Allah alone.

The greatest thing that Allah has forbidden is polytheism (*shirk*).

Polytheism is the worship of others along with Allah.

Sharia evidence for this is the Word of Allah Almighty:

"Say: "I have been ordered only to worship Allah and not to associate partners with Him" (Surah "ar - Ra'd", verse 36).

TOPIC FOR DISCUSSION

What is the name of the word that means to worship other than Allah?

Fill in the gaps with the appropriate words:

The greatest thing that Allah has commanded is

....

The greatest thing that Allah has forbidden is

....

Monotheism is the only way to happiness in this .... and in the next life.

Polytheism is the biggest cause for misfortune in this world and punishment in ....

Bring Sharia evidence indicating the obligatory worship of only one Allah!

Worship of Allah alone is the only way to happiness in this world and in the hereafter!

NOTES TO THE PARENT AND TEACHER:

Explain to the children that the mission of all the Prophets was the same: the call to monotheism and the prohibition of polytheism. As an example, give the stories of some Prophets, peace be upon them, which are narrated in the Quran.

Explain to the children the importance of monotheism! Explain to them that there is no other way to happiness in this world and in the Hereafter, except through monotheism!

Explain to your children the danger of polytheism! Explain to them that polytheism is the biggest cause for unhappiness in this world and punishment in the Hereafter. Therefore, Ibrahim, peace be upon him, turned to his Lord with the following prayer:

"Save me and my sons from worshiping idols!" (Surah Ibrahim, verse 35).

Give the children examples of some types of polytheism: sacrifice to other than Allah, oath not to Allah, wearing amulets, talismans, ropes, beads, etc. to ward off misfortune or protection from it.

Purpose of this lesson:

Explain to the children the greatness of monotheism.

Warn the children against polytheism, which is incompatible with monotheism.

Remind the children of the Shari'ah evidence indicating the obligatory worship of Allah alone.

Whoever worships other than Allah is a polytheist (*mushrik*). For example, the one who makes prayers not to Allah, or the one who sacrifices to someone other than Allah.

LESSON 15

Allah Almighty said: "Worship Allah and do not associate partners with Him!"

(Surah "an - Nisa", ayat 36).

TOPIC FOR DISCUSSION

Whoever worships other than Allah is a polytheist.

Give reference from the Quran or Authentic Hadeeth for this!

Give examples of polytheism!

Fill in the gaps with the appropriate words:

The punishment of a polytheist is eternal residence in
....

Whoever makes any kind of worship to other than Allah, for example, prayers and ...., then he is a polytheist.

Why does Satan strive to ensure that people fall into polytheism?

Polytheism is the cause of misfortune both in this world and in the Hereafter!

NOTES TO THE PARENT AND TEACHER:

Explain to the children that the one who turns any kind of worship not to Allah (for example, prayer, sacrifice, prostration, etc.) is a polytheist and an unbeliever, even if such a person prays, fasts, makes large and small pilgrimage (hajj and umrah) and believes that he is a Muslim.

Explain to the children that the first polytheists who lived at the time of the Messenger (peace and blessings of Allaah be upon him) performed some types of worship of Allah, but this did not bring them any benefit because of their polytheism. Explain to the children that the punishment for polytheism is an eternal stay in Hell. Allah Almighty said: "Verily, whoever associates partners with Allah, Allah has forbidden him Paradise. Hell will be his dwelling place, and the wicked will have no helpers!" (Surah "al - Maidah", verse 72).

Explain to the children the hostility of Satan towards people and his desire that a person falls into polytheism and misguidance, so that people find themselves together with Satan in Hell.

Purpose of this lesson:

Warn the children against polytheism.

Tell the children about some types of polytheism.

Clarify to the children about the Sharia judgment regarding the one who dedicated any worship to other than Allah.

Give the children reference from the Quran or Authentic Hadeeth that worship other than Allah is polytheism.

Write in order the three basics that a person should know:

1   –   Knowledge   of   the   slave   about
....

2   –   Knowledge   of   the   slave   about
....

3   -   Knowledge   of   the   slave   about
....

Name the signs of Allah and His creations that are mentioned in the following blessed verse:

Allah Almighty said: "Verily, in the creation of the heavens and the earth, as well as in the change of night and day, there are signs for those who have understanding" (Surah Aali - Imran, verse 190).

Fill in the gaps with the appropriate words:

Wisdom in the creation of jinn and people by Allah is that they ....

Whoever worships other than Allah is doing ....

The greatest thing that Allah has commanded is
....

The greatest thing that Allah has forbidden is
....

Three basics:

- The knowledge of the slave about his Lord

- Slave's knowledge of his religion

– Knowledge of a slave about his Prophet (peace and blessings of Allah be upon him)

LESSON 16

There are three levels of religion:

First Degree - Islam

Second Degree - Iman

Third Degree - Ihsan

The first step is Islam.

Islam is the worship of only Allah alone and submission to Him, as well as the rejection of disobedience to Him.

I am a Muslim; I love my Islamic religion and I am proud of it.

TOPIC FOR DISCUSSION

Complete the following definition with the appropriate words:

Islam is the worship of only Allah alone and............, as well as the rejection of ....

NOTES TO THE PARENT AND TEACHER:

Plant love for Islam and pride in this religion in the souls of the children.

Explain that Islam provides happiness, peace and opening of the chest (to the truth), while polytheism and misguidance are the greatest causes of chest tightness.

Allah Almighty has said:

"Whoever follows My guidance will not be misguided and miserable. And whoever turns away from My Reminder, a hard life awaits him, and on the Day of Resurrection We will resurrect him blind" (Surah "Ta Ha", verses 123-124).

Tell the children about some people who converted to Islam and found rest and tranquility in the breadth of this religion.

Purpose of this lesson:

Explain to the children the stages of religion.

Explain to the children the meaning of the word "Islam".

To instill in the children a sense of pride in the Islamic religion.

LESSON 17

Islam consists of five pillars:

The first pillar: witness that there is none worthy of worship except Allah and that Muhammad is the Messenger of Allah.

The Second Pillar: Prayer

The Third Pillar: Paying Zakat

The Fourth Pillar: Fasting the Month of Ramadan

The Fifth pillar: making the pilgrimage to Makkah, for the who has the opportunity and the means.

TOPIC FOR DISCUSSION

How many pillars of Islam are there?

Underline the words referring to the pillars of Islam:

Fasting in the month of Ramadan. Respect for parents. Hajj to Makkah, for the one who has the opportunity. Reading the Blessed Quran. Making a prayer. Witness that there is no one worthy of worship except Allah, and that Muhammad is the Messenger of Allah. Payment of zakat.

Complete the following sentence:

There are five pillars of Islam related to each other. A person must observe them in order to enter Paradise.

NOTES TO THE PARENT AND TEACHER:

Explain to the children the meaning of the word "pillar" (*rukn*) by giving an appropriate example. Explain to the children that Islam is confessed and affirmed only when the five pillars are observed.

Confirm the obligation of these pillars from Allah by quoting the hadeeth of the Prophet (peace and blessings of Allah be upon him): "Islam is based on five (pillars)…" (narrated by Muslim in his Sahih, No. 16).

Encourage the children to pray in a timely manner by explaining that prayer is the first deed for which the servant of Allah will be asked on the Day of Resurrection, as the Messenger of Allah (peace and blessings of Allah be upon him) said: "Verily, the first thing for which the servant (of Allah) will be asked on the Day of Resurrection from his deeds is prayer. If it was okay, then he would succeed and be saved. If not, then he will fail and suffer damage. (Narrated by - Tirmidhi, No. 413).

Warn the children against abandoning prayer and make it clear to them that those who left the prayer, fell into disbelief, as the Messenger of Allah (peace and blessings of Allah be upon him) said: "The covenant between us and them (the disbelievers) is prayer. Whoever left it fell into disbelief." (Narrated by - Tirmidhi, No. 2621).

Purpose of this lesson:

Remind the children that Islam has five pillars.

Clarify to the children the Sharia judgment on the fulfillment of these five pillars.

Explain to the children the importance of prayer and the obligation of its steady performance.

The meaning of *La ilaha illa - Allah*: There is no one worthy of worship except Allah.

The meaning of the testimony of Muhammadan rasulu - Allah: Muhammad is the Messenger of Allah.

Submission to Allah in what He ordered. Faith in what He said.

Keeping away from what He forbade. Worship Allah only as He decreed.

TOPIC FOR DISCUSSION

Fill in the gaps with the appropriate words:

a) I am a Muslim. I testify that ...., and that Muhammad ....

b) The meaning of *La ilaha illa - Allah*:

What is the meaning of the testimony of Muhammad is the Messenger of Allah?

Write three things that the Messenger of Allah (peace and blessings of Allah be upon him) ordered us:

1 - Prayer

2 -

3 -

4 -

Through the recognition and pronunciation in Arabic of the two testimonies, a person enters the Islamic religion!

NOTES TO THE PARENT AND TEACHER:

Explain to the children the great significance of the two testimonies of confession of faith through which a person enters Islam.

Point out to the children that there are people who falsely worship others with Allah. For example, one who makes prayers or makes sacrifices to the graves of the Prophets and the righteous. This refers to the great polytheism which Allah and His Messenger have forbidden.

Explain to the children that the testimony of La ilaha illa - Allah will benefit the person pronouncing it only if he knows its meaning, begins to act in accordance with its requirements, and if he protect himself from what things and actions that make it invalid.

Explain to the children that the best remembrance of Allah is the words of *La ilaha illa - Allah*. The one whose last words in this world will be *La ilaha illa - Allah* will go to Paradise.

Explain to the children in detail the meaning of the testimony that Muhammad is the Messenger of Allah:

a) obedience to him (peace and blessings of Allah be upon him) in what he ordered: performing the pillars of Islam and its obligatory deeds, for example, prayer, etc.

b) belief in what he said: for example, about the coming of the Hour of Judgment, Paradise, Hell, etc.

c) the removal of what he forbade and what he warned against: i.e., from major sins and minor sins. The greatest of the major sins is polytheism.

d) worshiping Allah only in the way He has decreed: i.e., performance of deeds of obedience and keeping away from religious innovations, like celebrating the birthday of the Prophet (*mawlid*).

Purpose of this lesson:

Explain to the children with us the verbal meaning of the words *La ilaha illa - Allah*.

To explain to the children with the help of Muhammad - the Messenger of Allah.

To inspire the children with love for the Messenger (peace and blessings of Allah be upon him) and to obey him.

Warn the children against what is contrary to the order of the Messenger (peace and blessings of Allah be upon him).

LESSON 18

Iman (faith) consists of six pillars:

Faith in Allah.

Faith in His angels.

Faith in His Scriptures.

Faith in His Messengers.

Faith in Judgment Day.

Faith in predestination, both good and bad.

TOPIC FOR DISCUSSION

How many pillars of *Iman* are there?

In each circle denoting the pillar of iman, put the corresponding number in order:

( ) Belief in Allah
( ) Belief in the Heavenly Scriptures
( ) Belief in Angels
( ) Belief in the Day of Judgment
( ) Belief in Messengers
( ) Belief in Predestination, both good and bad

The Almighty said: "He has ordained for you of religion what He enjoined upon Noah and that which

We have revealed to you, [O Muhammad], and what We enjoined upon Abraham and Moses and Jesus..." (Surah Ash-Shura, verse 13)

The Almighty also said: "Muhammad is the Messenger of Allah" (Surah Al-Fath, verse 29)

Write down the names of the Prophets who are mentioned in these two verses:

1)...

2)...

3)...

4)...

5)...

Through faith in these six pillars of iman, a person becomes happy in this world and in the Hereafter.

NOTES FOR THE PARENT AND TEACHER:

Explain to the children the meaning of the word *"iman"* (faith), and this is conviction in the heart, pronouncing with the tongue and doing deeds with the organs of the body. Explain to the children the well-known hadith of *Jibril*, peace be upon him, in which, in particular, it is said: "And tell me about iman!" (The Prophet) replied: "(Iman is) that you believe in Allah, in His angels, in His Scriptures, on the Day of

Judgment and in predestination, both good from it and bad" (narrated by Muslim in his Sahih No. 8).

Explain to the children that a person's happiness in this world and in the Hereafter is to believe in these six pillars of iman.

Explain to the children that the signs of faith include:
Love for Allah and obedience to Him.
The realization that Allah is constantly watching over us and knows all our hidden and obvious.
Memorizing the Qur'an by heart, meditating on its verses and doing deeds in accordance with them.
Preparation for the Day of Judgment through the performance of good deeds.
Contentment with the predestination of Allah.

Mention the names of some of the Prophets, angels, and also the names of the Scriptures which Allah sent down.

Teach the children some expressions that indicate the ordinance and predestination of Allah. For example, **qaddar - Allahu wa ma shaa fa'al** (Allah predestined this, and what He wished happened).

Explain to the children the need for faith in these six pillars of iman, and also that the denial of even one of these pillars of *iman* makes a person an unbeliever.

Purpose of this lesson:

- The children must list all six pillars of *iman*.

- Explain to the children the Sharia judgment about faith in these six pillars.

Explain to the children that faith is belief, word and deed.

Belief in resurrection after death refers to belief in the Day of Judgment

The meaning of the word "resurrection" (*al – ba's*) is that Allah will revive people after their death and bring them out of their graves for accounting and retribution.

Sharia judgment about belief in predestination. Faith in this is obligatory (*wajib*).

The Almighty said: "We created you from it (the earth), We will return you to it and take you out of it again" (Surah "Ta Ha", ayat 55).

LESSON 19

Sharia judgment about the one who denies resurrection after death. Such a person is a disbeliever in Allah Almighty.

TOPIC FOR DISCUSSION

Who will revive people after their death?

Fill in the gaps with the appropriate words:

Belief in resurrection after death, and the one who denies it, according to the Shari'ah is that he is a
....

One of the manifestations of the power of Allah Almighty is that He will resurrect people after their death for a great cause. What is this great thing?

The one to whom his book will be given in his right hand on the Day of Resurrection, will be among the successful and will receive an easy accounting. The one to whom his book will be handed in his left hand will be among the unfortunate and will receive a heavy accounting.

NOTES FOR THE PARENT AND TEACHER:

Affirm in the souls of the children the obligatory belief in the Day of Judgment, in resurrection after death, in accounting (of deeds) and in retribution. Tell them about some of the horrors of the Day of Judgment, and also that Allah will protect His servants who worship Him Alone from this, citing as examples the verses that the children have already studied, for example: "He who is given his book in his right hand will receive easy calculation" (Surah "al - Inshiqaq", verses 7-8).

Plant in the souls of the children the sprouts of the need to prepare for what will happen after death.

Affirm in the souls of the children the reality of the resurrection from the graves after death and show the children the greatness of Allah Almighty, Who is able to do so.

Purpose of this lesson:

- Explain to the children the meaning of the word "resurrection".

- Explain to the children the Sharia judgment of faith in resurrection after death.

- Explain to the children the Sharia judgment regarding the one who denies the resurrection after death.

LESSON 20

Ihsan is to worship Allah as if you see Him, and if you do not see Him, then, indeed, He sees you.

Sharia evidence for this is the following Words of Allah Almighty:

"Indeed, Allah is with those who fear Him and with those who perform *ihsan* (*muhsinun*)" (Surah an - Nahl, verse 128).

TOPIC FOR DISCUSSION

Fill in the gaps with the appropriate words:

Ihsan is .... as if you see Him, and if ...., then, indeed, He sees you.

The third step of the steps of religion is .... and it is the highest of them.

Give Shari'ah evidence indicating *ihsan*:

....
....

A sincere believer will never steal, even if no one sees him. Why?

I know that Allah is always watching me, so I do not commit sins either secretly or in front of everyone.

I perform the rites of worship, striving for the pleasure of Allah Almighty

NOTES FOR THE PARENT AND TEACHER:

Explain to the children that *ihsan* is the highest level of religion.

Explain to the children that the performance of worship in the best way is *ihsan*.

Encourage the children to develop a sense of that Allah Almighty is always watching over His servants. So, the Almighty said: "Verily, Allah is watching over you" (Surah "an - Nisa", ayat 1).

Tell the children some stories from the life of the righteous, in which they reported how they felt that Allah was watching them. An example is the story of Umar ibn al - Khattab, may Allah be pleased with him, and one girl who refused to dilute milk with water out of fear of Allah.

Purpose of this lesson:

1 - Explain to the children the meaning of the word "Ihsan".

2 - Give the children Sharia evidence for ihsan.

3 - Encourage the children to sincerely worship Allah.

LESSON 21

The three foundations are:

1 - The slave's knowledge of his Lord

2 - The slave's knowledge of his religion

3 - Knowledge of a slave about his Prophet (peace and blessings of Allah be upon him)

Prophet Muhammad, son of Abdullah, son of Abdul - Muttalib, son of Hashim. The Hashim are from the Quraysh tribe, and the Quraysh are from the Arabs.

Prophet Muhammad (peace and blessings of Allah be upon him) is the seal of the Prophets.

Sharia evidence for this is the following Words of Allah Almighty:

"Muhammad is not the father of any of your men, but is the Messenger of Allah and the seal (last) of the Prophets. Allah knows about everything" (Surah "al - Ahzab", ayat 40).

The Sharia judgment of love and obedience to the Prophet, peace and blessings of Allah be upon him, is that it (loving and obeying him) is obligatory (wajib) for every Muslim.

TOPIC FOR DISCUSSION

Fill in the gaps with the appropriate words:

Prophet Muhammad, son of ...., son of Abdul Muttalib, son of ....

To love the Messenger of Allah, peace and blessings of Allah be upon him, and to obey him according to the Shariah judgment is ....

The seal of the Prophets is ....

The Prophet, peace and blessings of Allah be upon him, said: "More often offer *salat* for me on Friday afternoon and Friday evening! Whoever offers *salat* for me once, for him Allah will offer *salat* ten times" (this hadith was narrated by al - Bayhaqi in his collection "as - Sunan" 3/249).

Read this hadeeth and answer the following questions:

On what day is it recommended to offer *salat* and *salam* more often for the Messenger of Allah, peace and blessings of Allah be upon him?

Together with your parent, remember some story that tells about the love of the Companions, may Allah be pleased with them, for the Prophet, peace and blessings of Allah be upon him.

I love the Messenger of Muhammad, peace and blessings of Allah be upon him, and obey him.

NOTES FOR THE PARENT AND TEACHER:

Briefly review with the children the first and second foundations of religion and establish the connection of these two foundations with the third foundation.

Prepare for this lesson so that you can explain to the children in what ignorance and misguidance most people were before the advent of the Prophet Muhammad, peace and blessings of Allah be upon him.

Explain to the children the noble life of the Messenger of Allah, peace be upon him and blessings of Allah.

Explain to the children the expression "seal of the Prophets" - that Muhammad, peace and blessings of Allah be upon him, was the last of them, and there will be no Prophet after him.

Explain to the children the need for love for the Prophet, peace be upon him and the blessings of Allah, without showing excess in this and without going beyond the boundaries, which include turning to him with prayers or turning to him for help (only Allah alone deserves our worship and we must turn to only Allah alone with our prayers).

Explain to the children that love for the Prophet, peace and blessings of Allah be upon him, requires us to obey him and follow him in his words and in his deeds.

Encourage the children to offer *salat* for the Prophet, peace and blessings of Allah be upon him, because of the great reward that is promised to the one who will do this, especially regarding the offering of *salat* after mentioning the name of the Prophet, peace and blessings of Allah be upon him.

Purpose of this lesson:

- Remind the children of the genealogy of the Prophet, peace and blessings of Allah be upon him.

- Instill in the children love for the Messenger of Allah, peace and blessings of Allah be upon him, and obedience to him.

- Bring the Sharia evidence to the children, indicating that the Prophet Muhammad, peace and blessings of Allah be upon him, is the seal of the Prophets.

- *Salat* from Allah is the praise of a slave in the highest company of close angels.

And in conclusion, praise be to Allah - the Lord of the worlds!

Peace and blessings be upon our Prophet Muhammad, his family members and all his companions!

LESSON 22

In the Name of Allah, the Most Merciful, the Most Merciful to the believers!

Write down three basics that every person should know and act in accordance with:

Slave's knowledge of ....

Slave's knowledge of his religion

Slave's knowledge of ....

Write to the end in order all the pillars of faith:

You should believe in Allah, in ...., in His Scriptures, in.., on Judgment Day, and in ....

Answer the following questions:

1 - What is the name of the first pillar of Islam?

2 - Who is the seal of the Prophets?

3 - What is *ihsan*?

Religion has three levels, namely:

1 - Islam

2 – Iman

3 – Ihsan

The first step is ISLAM

The meaning of the word "ISLAM":

Submission to Allah through monotheism, submission to Him through obedience and renunciation of polytheism and polytheists.

Explanation of the meaning of the word "ISLAM":

Submission to Allah through monotheism is worship of Allah alone.

Submission to Him through obedience is doing what Allah has commanded and refusing what He has forbidden.

Renunciation of polytheism and polytheists is hatred for polytheism and a firm conviction of its falsity, as well as dislike for polytheists.

TOPIC FOR DISCUSSION

Write the definition of the word "Islam".

He who does good deeds will prosper in this world, having a good and peaceful life, and in the next life, enter Paradise.

NOTES FOR THE PARENT AND TEACHER:

Point out to the children that Jibril, peace be upon him, asked the Messenger of Allah, peace and blessings of Allah be upon him, about these three steps of religion, which Muslim reported in his Sahih (No. 8).

Explain to the children the linguistic meaning of the word "Islam" comes from the word musalama (peace, reconciliation), i.e. leaving strife. In the same way, a Muslim (muslim) is one who submits (mustaslim) to the orders of Allah, obeying Him through obedience and renouncing polytheism and polytheists.

Explain to the children that the fruits of obedience to Allah and submission.

Through obedience to Him: a good and happy life in this world, gaining success through the pleasure of Allah, entering Paradise and salvation from Hell.

Tell the children the story of Ibrahim, peace be upon him, and his fellow tribesmen, how he renounced polytheism and polytheists, how he showed enmity towards them, and how he urged them to follow him.

Allah Almighty said:

"Ibrahim and those who were with him were a wonderful example for you. They said to their people: 'We renounce you and those whom you worship instead of Allah. We reject you, and enmity and hatred have been established between us and you forever, until you believe in Allah alone' (Surah al-Mumtahina, verse 4).

Explain to the children that hatred of polytheism and polytheists does not mean injustice to them and the commission of violence against them. One can cooperate with them in worldly affairs.

Give some examples of renunciation of polytheists: hatred for them and the desire not to be like them.

Explain also their false beliefs and explain that the only true religion is Islam.

Purpose of this lesson:

- Explain to the children the three stages of religion.
- Explain to the children the meaning of the word "Islam".
- Give the children some examples of renunciation of polytheists.

There are five pillars of Islam:

- evidence that there is no one worthy of worship except Allah, and that Muhammad is the Messenger of Allah.
- performing a prayer.

- payment of zakat.
- fasting in the month of Ramadan.
- Hajj to the House of Allah, for the one who has the opportunity.

Sharia evidence for these five pillars is contained in the words of the Prophet, peace and blessings of Allah be upon him:

"Islam is based on five (pillars): bearing witness that there is none worthy of worship except Allah and that Muhammad is the Messenger of Allah, praying, paying zakat, fasting Ramadan and performing Hajj to the House (of Allah). (Al-Bukhari and Muslim).

TOPIC FOR DISCUSSION

Write to the end all the pillars of Islam:

(1) witness that there is none worthy of worship except Allah, and that Muhammad is the Messenger of Allah.

(2) ....

(3) paying zakat.

(4) ....

(5) ....

Fill in the gaps with the appropriate words:

Allah does not accept any other religion except

....

The first pillar of Islam is

....

Give Sharia evidence from the Sunnah regarding the pillars of Islam.

Islam is the only reason for entering Paradise and escaping from Hell.

NOTES FOR THE PARENT AND TEACHER:

Explain to the children that these pillars of Islam are the foundation without which the religion cannot stand, because the building also cannot stand without the foundation and supports.

Explain to the children that one of the fruits of practicing Islam is the inviolability of the life of a Muslim and his property. The Messenger of Allah, peace and blessings of Allah be upon him, said: I was ordered to fight people until they say: La ilaha illa-Allah (There is none worthy of worship except Allah!) The same who says: "La ilaha illa-Allah", thereby protecting his property and his life from me, unless (he does anything for which he can be deprived of his property or life) by right, and then (only) Allah will make a settlement with him" (this narrated by al-Bukhari, no. 2946).

Explain to the children that Islam is the only reason for entering into Paradise and salvation from Hell, and that Allah does not accept any other religion. Allah Almighty said: "From the one who seeks a religion other than Islam, this will never be accepted, and in the Hereafter he will be among those who suffered loss" (Surah Aali Imran, ayat 85).

Tell the children the stories of some people, both past and present who, having embraced Islam, found happiness and strength through the practice of this great religion.

It is reported that Umar ibn al-Khattab, may Allah be pleased with him, said: "We are a people that Allah has exalted through Islam. And if we were striving for greatness through something else, then Allah would certainly humiliate us."

Purpose of this lesson:

- Children should be able to list the five pillars of Islam.

- Bring the reference from the Quran or Authentic Hadeeth to the children on the pillars of Islam.

- Explain to the children the importance of these five pillars of religion.

LESSON 23

WITNESS THAT THERE IS NO ONE WORTHY OF WORSHIP BUT ALLAH AND THAT MUHAMMAD IS THE MESSENGER OF ALLAH.

WITNESS THAT THERE IS NO ONE WORTHY OF WORSHIP EXCEPT ALLAH.

The Shari'ah evidence for the obligatory witness that there is no one worthy of worship except Allah is contained in the following Words of the Almighty:

"Allah has testified that there is none worthy of worship except Him, as well as the angels and those who have knowledge. He supports justice. There is no one worthy of worship except Him, the Mighty, the Wise" (Surah Aali Imran, ayat 18).

The meaning of the words LA ILAHA ILLA ALLAH:

There is no one who is rightfully deserving of worship except Allah.

TOPIC FOR DISCUSSION

Emphasize the first of the five pillars of Islam: testimony that there is no one worthy of worship except Allah, and that Muhammad is the Messenger of Allah.

Give Sharia evidence for the obligatory witness that there is no one worthy of worship except Allah.

What is the meaning of the words: "La ilaha illa-Allah"?

Fill in the gaps with the appropriate words:

The key to Paradise is ………………………………

Prepare a lesson with the children on the topic: "On the virtues of pronouncing the words: "La ilaha illa-Allah."

The best remembrance of Allah is the words: LA ILAHA ILLA-ALLAH

NOTES FOR THE PARENT AND TEACHER:

Explain to the children that the one who will say: "La ilaha illa-Allah" and act in accordance with the prescription of these words will enter Paradise.

Explain to the children that the one who dedicates at least one kind of worship to other than Allah, for example, calling with a supplication, is a polytheist, even if such a person pronounces: "La ilaha illa-Allah", because the essence of monotheism is the dedication of worship to Allah alone.

Explain to the children that the key to Paradise is the words: "La ilaha illa-Allah." Each key must have teeth. The prongs of the key to Paradise are the fulfillment of what is commanded and the abstaining from what is forbidden.

Explain to the children that the words of monotheism: "La ilaha illa-Allah" are the best remembrance of Allah, as the Messenger of Allah, peace and blessings of Allah be upon him, said: "The best words of remembrance of Allah are La ilaha illa-Allah" (this hadith was narrated by at-Tirmidhi, No. 3383).

Explain to children that the first thing to encourage non-believers to say is that there is no one worthy of worship except Allah, as reported in the hadith of the Messenger of Allah, peace and blessings of Allah be upon him, when he sent Muadh to Yemen as a judge and mentor.

The Prophet, peace and blessings of Allah be upon him, said to him:

"Indeed, you will come to a people from among the People of the Book. When you come to them, then call them to testify that there is no one worthy of worship except Allah! (Narrated by al-Bukhari, no. 4347).

Explain to the children the great virtue of calling to Allah. Messenger of Allah, peace and blessings of Allah be upon him, said: "If through you Allah guides at least one person to the true path, then it will be better for you than the most selective property (literally, the hadith says "than red camels")" (narrated by al-Bukhari (no. 3701) and Muslim (2406).

Purpose of this lesson:

- Explain to the children the first pillar of Islam.

- Give the children Sharia evidence for the words: "La ilaha illa-Llah".

- Explain to the children the meaning of the words: "La ilaha illa-Llah."

LESSON 24

WITNESS THAT MUHAMMAD IS THE MESSENGER OF ALLAH

The meaning of the testimony of Muhammad is the Messenger of Allah:

- Submission to the Prophet (peace and blessings of Allah be upon him) in what he ordered.

- Trusting him in what he said.

- Detachment from what he forbade and what he warned against.

- Worship Allah only in the way he has established.

The Sharia evidence for the obligatory evidence that Muhammad is the Messenger of Allah is contained in the following Words of the Almighty:

"Muhammad is not the father of any of you men, but is the Messenger of Allah and the seal of the Prophets. Allah knows about everything" (Surah "al-Ahzab", verse 40).

TOPIC FOR DISCUSSION

What is the meaning of the testimony: "Muhammad is the Messenger of Allah"?

Complete the sentences as in the first sentence:

a) The Messenger of Allah, peace and blessings of Allah be upon him, ordered us to obey Allah and forbade us to disobey Him.

b) The Messenger of Allah, peace and blessings of Allah be upon him, ordered us monotheism (tawhid) and forbade us ....

c) The Messenger of Allah, peace and blessings of Allah be upon him, ordered us to be truthful and forbade us

....

Give Shari'a evidence for the obligatory evidence that Muhammad is the Messenger of Allah.

Name a book about the life of the Prophet Muhammad, peace and blessings of Allah be upon him, which you would advise your children to read.

True love for the Messenger of Allah, peace and blessings of Allah be upon him, consists in obeying him in everything and steadily following him.

NOTES FOR THE PARENT AND TEACHER:

Explain to the children the obligatory obedience to the Messenger of Allah, peace and blessings of Allah be upon him, in what he ordered. Allah Almighty said: "Take what the Messenger gave you and avoid what he forbade you" (Surah al-Hashr, verse 7).

Encourage the children to believe what the Messenger said, peace and blessings of Allah be upon him, including about the affairs of the hidden, for example, about the onset of the Hour of Judgment, Paradise and Hell.

Warn the children against disobeying the Messenger of Allah, peace be upon him and blessings of Allah. So, Allah Almighty reported that the inhabitants of Hell will regret this omission and repent of it: "On that day, their faces will turn in Fire, and they will say: Oh, if only we obeyed Allah and obeyed the Messenger!" (al-Ahzab, verse 66).

Establish in the hearts of the children the obligatory worship of Allah (peace be upon him and the blessings of Allah) only as He ordered, and not to enter into religion any innovations, for which there is no command of Allah. For example, such religious innovations as the celebration of the night of the transfer of the Prophet from Makkah to Jerusalem and his ascension to heaven (al-isra wal-miraj), mother's day, birthday, etc. The Messenger of Allah, peace and blessings of Allah be upon him, said: "Every religious innovation is a misguidance." (this hadith was transmitted by Muslim, no. 867).

Explain to the children that true love for the Messenger of Allah, peace be upon him and the blessings of Allah, consists in obeying him in everything and steadily following him.

Mention some books about the life of the Messenger of Allah, peace be upon him and the blessings of Allah.

Purpose of this lesson:

- Explain to the children the meaning of the testimony: "Muhammad is the Messenger of Allah".

- Bring the reference from the Quran or Authentic Hadeeth to the obligatoriness to the children the testimony: "Muhammad is the Messenger of Allah".

- Warn the children against contradicting the Messenger of Allah, peace and blessings of Allah be upon him.

LESSON 25

Second Pillar - Prayer

Third Pillar - Pay Zakat

The meaning of the words: "Perform prayer" is the worship of Allah by performing five obligatory prayers at a strictly defined time in the way that the Prophet Muhammad, peace and blessings of Allah be upon him, explained.

The meaning of the words: "Paying zakat" is the worship of Allah by allocating part of your property and distributing it to those people who have the right to it.

Reference from the Quran or Authentic Hadeeth of the obligation of prayer and zakat is contained in the following Words of the Almighty:

"Perform prayer, pay zakat and bow down with those bowing down in the waist" (Surah al-Baqarah, verse 43).

Shariah judgment on who denies obligatory prayer or zakat:

Such a person is a disbeliever in Allah Almighty!

TOPIC FOR DISCUSSION

Give Sharia evidence for the obligation to perform prayer and pay zakat.

Underline the pillars of Islam that are mentioned in the following verse:

"But they were ordered only to worship Allah, serving him sincerely, like monotheists, to perform prayer and pay zakat. This is the right faith" (Surah "al-Bayyina", verse 5)

Write a two-line letter to your brother in which you encourage him to keep praying.

In the Name of Allah, the Most Gracious, the Most Gracious! To my brother:

Peace be upon you, the mercy of Allah and His blessings!

....

....

I pray regularly and on time.

I also know that not paying zakat is one of the reasons for not being blessed with rain.

NOTES FOR THE PARENT AND TEACHER:

Encourage class members to pray regularly and on time, and explain to them that the one who refuses to pray is an unbeliever. The Prophet, peace and blessings of Allah be upon him, said: "The covenant between us and them is prayer. Therefore, whoever left it (the prayer) became a disbeliever" (narrated by Ahmad, 5/346).

Explain to the children that paying zakat is the reason of blessings (baraka) of property, as well as consolation for the poor and needy. Also, make it clear to the children that not paying zakat is one of the reasons why it doesn't rain.

Purpose of this lesson:

- Remind the children about the second and third pillars of Islam.
- Encourage the children to pray constantly and in a timely manner.
- Bring the Sharia evidence to the children on the obligation of prayer and zakat.

LESSON 26

Fourth Pillar - Fasting in the month of Ramadan

The fifth pillar is the Hajj to the Protected House of Allah, for the one who has the opportunity.

The meaning of the word "fasting" is the worship of Allah by refraining from food, drink and some other things from the moment the dawn appears until the sunset.

The Sharia evidence for the obligatory fasting is contained in the following Words of the Almighty:

"O you who believe! Fasting is prescribed for you, just as it was prescribed for your predecessors - perhaps you will become God-fearing" (Surah al-Baqarah verse 183).

The meaning of the word "Hajj to the House of Allah" is the worship of Allah by setting off on a journey to His House at a certain time to perform certain rites of worship to Allah Almighty.

Sharia evidence for the obligation of the Hajj is contained in the following Words of the Almighty:

"People are obliged before Allah to perform Hajj to the House, who has the opportunity to do so" (Surah Al Imran, verse 97).

Sharia judgment about who denies the obligation of fasting or Hajj: Such a person is a disbeliever in Allah Almighty!

TOPIC FOR DISCUSSION

Complete the sentences with suitable words: Pillars of Islam:

The first pillar is the testimony that there is none worthy of worship except Allah and that Muhammad is the Messenger of Allah.

The fourth pillar -

....

....

Fifth pillar -

....

....

The Almighty said: "The night of predestination is better than a thousand months. On this night, the angels and the Spirit (Jibril) descend with the permission of their Lord, according to all His commands. It is prosperous until dawn" (Surah al-Qadr, verses 3-5).

(a) What month is the night of predestination in?

b) Describe the virtues of the night of destiny.

Give reference from the Quran or Authentic Hadeeth for obligatory Hajj.

Have you taken part in the evening meal after sunset (iftar) with those who fast in the month of Ramadan? Why did you do it?

How many times must a Muslim perform Hajj?

The Messenger of Allah, peace and blessings of Allah be upon him, reported to his companions the joyful news of the coming month of Ramadan and told them that in this month the gates of Paradise are opened and the gates of Hell are locked.

NOTES FOR THE PARENT AND TEACHER:

Encourage your children to fast during the month of Ramadan and explain to them the virtues of fasting. The Prophet, peace and blessings of Allah be upon him, said: "Whoever fasted in Ramadan with faith and hope (for the reward of Allah), his former sins will be forgiven" (this hadith was narrated by al-Bukhari (No. 38) and Muslim (No. 760).

Explain to the children that it is obligatory to perform the Hajj once in their life for those who have the opportunity.

Tell the children about the high position that the Protected House of Allah occupies in the souls of Muslims.

Purpose of this lesson:

- Remind the children about the fourth and fifth pillars of Islam.
- Explain to the children the virtues of fasting in the month of Ramadan.
- Provide the children with Sharia evidence for the obligation of fasting and Hajj.

Islam consists of five pillars. Write them in order:

The first pillar is the testimony that there is none worthy of worship except Allah, and that Muhammad is the Messenger of Allah.

The second pillar -

....
....

...

The third pillar -

....
....

...

Fourth pillar -

....
....

Fifth pillar -

....
....

....

Select one of the pillars of Islam from each Sharia evidence below:

a) "O you who believe! Fasting is prescribed for you, just as it was prescribed for your predecessors - perhaps you will become God-fearing "(Surah al-Baqarah, ayat 183).

b) "People are obliged before Allah to perform Hajj to the House, who has the opportunity to do so" (Surah Al Imran, ayat 97).

c) "Indeed, prayer is prescribed for believers at a strictly defined time" (Surah An-Nisa, ayat 103).

LESSON 27

Second step: IMAN

(Islam) (Iman) (Ihsan)

The meaning of the word "iman" is a firm conviction in the heart, pronunciation with the tongue and the performance of deeds by the organs of the body.

Iman consists of six pillars:

- Faith in Allah.
- Faith in His angels.
- Faith in His Scriptures.
- Faith in His Messengers.
- Belief in Judgment Day.
- Belief in predestination, both good and bad.

Whoever rejects at least one of these six pillars of iman, he will become a disbeliever in Allah Almighty!

Iman increases due to obedience to Allah and decreases due to disobedience to Him

TOPIC FOR DISCUSSION

What is the meaning of the word "iman"?

Write next to the pillar of iman a number that corresponds to the order of this pillar:

( ) Faith in Allah

( ) Faith in His Scriptures

( ) Faith in the Day of Judgment

( ) Faith in His angels

( ) Faith in His Messengers

( ) Belief in predestination, both good and bad

Write in the table three deeds related to obedience to Allah, due to which iman increases, as well as three sins, due to which iman decreases.

Deeds of obedience to Allah, due to which iman increases: Seeking forgiveness from Allah.

Sins due to which iman decreases: Falsehood (telling lies).

Whoever rejects at least one of the six pillars of iman, he will become ....

I hasten to perform such deeds of obedience to Allah, which increase my iman.

I also avoid committing sins that decrease my iman.

NOTES FOR THE PARENT AND TEACHER:

Prepare for the topic of this lesson by reviewing the three steps of religion.

Explain to the children that whoever denies even one of the six pillars of iman is an unbeliever.

As an example of increasing and decreasing iman, give the following statement of one of the righteous predecessors: "If we mention our Lord and fear Him, then this is an increase in iman. If we show carelessness, forgetfulness and negligence, then this is a decrease in iman."

Encourage the children to do more good deeds as they are the cause of the increase of iman and its strengthening.

Almighty said: "The only believers are those whose hearts are afraid at the mention of Allah, whose faith is strengthened when His verses are read to them, who trust in their Lord" (Surah al-Anfal, verse 2).

Warn class members against small sins and big sins, because they are the cause of the reduction of iman and its weakening. The Messenger of Allah, peace and blessings of Allah be upon him, said: "... when a thief steals, then at the time of theft he is not a believer" (this hadith was transmitted by al-Bukhari, No. 5578).

Purpose of this lesson:

1 - Explain to the children the meaning of the word "iman".

2 - Remind the children about the six pillars of iman.

3 - Explain to the children the Sharia judgment about a person who denies at least one of the pillars of iman.

LESSON 28

BELIEF IN ALLAH

The meaning of the words "Faith in Allah": Highlighting Allah alone in dominance, worship, Names and Attributes.

- The words: "The selection of Allah in dominion (*rububiya*)" means:

The statement that Allah is the Creator (al-Khaliq),

Giving means of subsistence (ar-Razzaq) and only He alone manages the affairs of all things.

I am Muslim. I believe that Allah created me, and He also created the heavens, the earth, people and jinn, and none other than Allah created them.

I believe that Allah Alone provides people with livelihood, birds and animals, and no one else keeps them alive. I believe that Allah will revive people after their death, as He created them for the first time, and no one else is able to do this except Allah Almighty!

- The words: "Isolation of Allah in worship (uluhiyya)" mean:

Dedication of all types of worship to Allah alone.

For example, making prayers to no one other than Allah, or sacrificing an animal to no one other than Allah.

I am Muslim. I only pray to Allah and do not pray to anyone else.

I only make prayers to Allah and I do not make prayers to no one else besides Him. I rely only on Allah and I don't rely on anyone else.

– The words: "The Emphasis of Allah in the Names and Attributes" means:

The affirmation of the Names of Allah and His Attributes as they are said in the Qur'an, and the belief that there is nothing like Him from His creations.

I am Muslim. I believe in all the Names of Allah.

For example, ar-Rahman (All-Merciful), as-Sami' (All-Hearing), al-Qawuyyy (Strong), al-'Alim (All-knowing).

I also believe in all the Attributes of Allah.

For example, ar-Rahma (Grace), as-Sam' (Hearing), al-Quwwa (Strength), al-'Ilm (Knowledge).

TOPIC FOR DISCUSSION

What is the meaning of the words: "Faith in Allah"?

Explain the meaning of the words: "Singling out Allah in worship."

Underline the Names of Allah Almighty and His Attributes in the following verses:
"Will He Who created not know this, if He is the Insightful, the Knower?" (Surah Al-Mulk, verse 14).

"Verily, the mercy of Allah is close to those who do good" (Surah al-A'raf, verse 56).

"Say: "The knowledge of this is with Allah, and I am only a warning and clarifying exhorter" (Surah al-Mulk, verse 26).

"Say: "He is Allah the One" (Surah al-Ikhlas, verse 1).

Read the last verse from Surah al-Hashr (Surah 59) and write down the five Names of Allah Almighty.

1)...

2)...

3)...

4)...

5)...

I am a believer and I worship only Allah Alone!

NOTES FOR THE PARENT AND TEACHER:

Explain to the children that the recognition of dominion of Allah alone is not enough for a slave of Allah to enter Islam. No, you also need to worship Allah alone so that all types of worship are directed only to Allah alone. After all, the polytheists at the time of the Messenger of Allah, peace and blessings of Allah be upon him, recognized the dominance of Allah, but this did not make them Muslims, although they performed different types of worship, such as Hajj, Umrah, watering pilgrims, circumambulating the Kaaba. All this did not help them, because they associated partners with Allah, and because of this, their good deeds became invalid.

Point out to the children that he who does not worship only the One Allah alone, falls into great polytheism, which entails such a punishment from Allah Almighty, which does not entail any other sin. Allah Almighty said: "Verily, whoever associates partners with Allah, He has forbidden Paradise. Hellfire will be his refuge, and the wrongdoers will have no helpers" (Surah Al-Maida, verse 72).

Compare the greatness and honor of the life of a believer with the contemptible and insignificant existence of an unbeliever, whose life is like cattle, about which the Almighty said: "But the unbelievers enjoy the benefits and eat like cattle. Fire will be their abode" (Surah Muhammad, verse 12).

Belief in the Names and Attributes of Allah is one of the reasons for the increase in iman. The heart of the one who believes that Allah is All-Knowing (al-'Alim), ar-Rakib (Watcher), will be filled with the feeling that Allah is constantly watching over us, whether we are in motion or at rest.

Explain to the children that denying even one of the Names or Attributes of Allah is disbelief, as the Almighty said: "And they did not believe in the All-Merciful" (Surah al-Ra'd, verse 30).

Purpose of this lesson:

- Explain to the children the meaning of the words: "Faith in Allah".

- Warn the children against turning any kind of worship other than to Allah.

- Give the children examples of some of the Names and Attributes of Allah.

LESSON 29

BELIEF IN ANGELS

The words "faith in angels" mean:

A firm belief in the existence of angels, and also in the fact that Allah created them to worship Him. They (the angels) do not disobey Allah in what He has commanded them, and do what they are commanded to do.

Sharia evidence for belief in angels is contained in the following Words of the Almighty:

"The Messenger and the believers believed in what was sent down to him from the Lord. They all believed in Allah, His angels, His Scriptures and His Messengers" (Surah "al-Baqarah", ayat 285).

The number of angels is large, and among them are such as:

1 - Jibril, peace be upon him (alayhi salam).

2 - Mikhail, peace be upon him (alayhi salam).

3 - Israfil, peace be upon him (alayhi salam).

Sharia judgment about who denies the existence of angels: Such a person is a disbeliever in Allah Almighty!

TOPIC FOR DISCUSSION

Do the pillars of iman include "belief in angels"? What is the meaning of this faith?

Underline the names of the angels:

Ibrahim

Jibril

Mikhail

Muhammad

Israfil

Give two qualities of angels.

Name the angels who occupy the highest position?

I believe angels record a person's deeds, both good and bad!

NOTES FOR THE PARENT AND TEACHER:

Explain to the children that the highest position among all the angels is occupied by Jibril, peace be upon him, who was entrusted with the task of Revelation. Israfil is entrusted with blowing the Horn, and Mikhail is entrusted with responsibility for the rain.

Explain to the children some of the activities of angels and the consequences of believing in them:

They are instructed to record the affairs of people. This obliges the servant of Allah not to say or do anything that can cause the wrath of Allah Almighty.

They are instructed to protect the servant of Allah in different life circumstances. This obliges the servant of Allah to thank the Almighty for His concern for people.

They are instructed to take the souls of people. This obliges the servant of Allah to prepare for the Day of Judgment by doing good deeds.

Purpose of this lesson:

- Explain to the children the meaning of the words "faith in angels".

- Bring the Sharia evidence to the children on the obligatory belief in angels.

- Mention to the children some names of angels.

- Explain to the children the Sharia judgment about the one who does not believe in angels.

LESSON 30

BELIEF IN SCRIPTURES AND MESSENGERS

The words "faith in the Scriptures" mean:

The firm belief that Allah sent down the Books to His Messengers as a guide for people.

The Greatest Scripture is the Blessed Qur'an, which is the Word of Allah Almighty.

The words "faith in Messengers" mean:

A firm belief that Allah sent Messengers to His creations and that they were truthful in what they reported.

The call of all the Prophets was the same: the command to worship only Allah alone (tawhid) and the prohibition of polytheism (shirk).

The first Messenger was Nuh (Noah), peace be upon him, and the last of them was Muhammad, peace and blessings of Allah be upon him.

There were many other Prophets and Messengers between these two Messengers.

The best of the Messengers were five, who are called "possessors of firm determination" (ulu-l-'azm):

- Nuh (Noah), peace be upon him.

- Ibrahim (Abraham), peace be upon him.

- Musa (Moses), peace be upon him.

- Isa (Jesus), peace be upon him.

- Muhammad, peace and blessings be upon him.

Shari'ah evidence for belief in the Scriptures and Messengers is contained in the following words of the Almighty:

"The Messenger and the believers believed in what was sent down to him from the Lord. They all believed in Allah, His angels, His Books and His Messengers."

(al-Baqarah, verse 285)

TOPIC FOR DISCUSSION

Fill in the blanks with the appropriate words:

The greatest Scripture is ....

The first Messenger is ....

The last Messenger is ....

The call of the Prophets is one. What is this call?

Give Sharia evidence for the obligatory belief in the Scriptures and Messengers.

With your help let the child list the names of the Messengers who are called "possessors of firm determination", in the order according to which they were sent with their message.

I am Muslim. I love the Quran, read it and act in accordance with it! I also love all the Messengers because they wanted to guide people to the right path!

NOTES FOR THE PARENT AND TEACHER:

Explain to the children the mercy of Allah to people, which consists in the fact that He sent Messengers to them and sent down the Scriptures to show them the true path.

Mention some of the Scriptures that Allah revealed to His Messengers. For example, Taurat (Torah) and Injil (Gospel), which, however, were distorted later (by humans) in contrast to the Holy Qur'an, for the preservation of which, in an unchanged form, Allah vouched for, saying: "Verily, We have sent down the Reminder, and We protect it" (Surah "al-Hijr", ayat 9).

Explain to the children the virtues of the Blessed Quran, and encourage them to read it, memorize it, and act on it. Explain to class members that faith in all Messengers and Prophets is required. The first Messenger was Nuh, peace be upon him, and the last of them was Muhammad, peace and blessings of Allah be upon him, who is the best Prophet and Messenger. There were many other Prophets between these two Messengers. Some of them we know about, and some we don't.

Explain to the children that all Messengers were human and created by Allah. They have no signs of dominance or divinity, they did not know the secret (Ghayb), and they did not manage the affairs of the universe.

Explain to the children that one who claims that there is a Prophet after the Last Prophet – peace and blessings of Allah be upon him, is a disbeliever, and whoever believes it is also a disbeliever, for there is no more Prophet after Prophet Muhammad, peace and blessings of Allah be upon him. Allah Almighty said: "Muhammad is not the father of any of you men, but is the Messenger of Allah and the seal of the Prophets. Allah knows about everything" (Surah "al-Ahzab", verse 40).

Tell the stories of some of the Prophets and their people. For example, history of Nuh and Ibrahim, peace be upon them both.

Purpose of this lesson:

- Explain to the children the meaning of "faith in the Scriptures and Messengers".

- Explain to the children that the Blessed Quran is the Word of Allah Almighty.

- Explain to the children the Sharia judgment about who denies the Scriptures and the Messengers.

- Explain to the children that Allah revealed the Qur'an to Muhammad, peace and blessings of Allah be upon him.

LESSON 31

BELIEF IN JUDGMENT DAY

The words "belief in the Day of Judgment" mean:

A firm belief in everything that happens after death, as reported in the Qur'an and Sunnah.

Sharia evidence for belief in the Day of Judgment is contained in the following Words of the Almighty:

"... and in the last life they are convinced" (Surah "al-Baqarah", ayat 4).

What happens after death includes:

- The questions of the angels to the servant of Allah in his grave about the three basics: Who is your Lord? What is your religion? Who is your Prophet?

- Bliss in the grave or punishment in it (based on a person's answer to these questions in his grave).

- Resurrection. This is the exodus of people from their graves for accounting and retribution, so that the inhabitants of Paradise enter Paradise, and the inhabitants of Hell enter Fire.

- Calculation for deeds.

Sharia judgment about who denies the Day of Judgment: Such a person is a disbeliever in Allah Almighty!

TOPIC FOR DISCUSSION

Mention two events that will take place after death.

Put the following phrases in order to end up with a definition of the word "Resurrection":

for calculation and retribution.

that the inhabitants of Paradise may enter Paradise.

from their graves.

and the inhabitants of Hell entered the Fire

The resurrection is the exodus of people..

....

....

Regarding what happens after death, there are three questions that are asked to the servant of Allah in his grave. List them.

I am Muslim. I prepare for the Day of Judgment by doing good deeds.

NOTES FOR THE PARENT AND TEACHER:

Explain to the children that the Day of Judgment has many names, such as the Day of Resurrection (Yawm al-Qiyamah), the Striking (al-Qari'a), the Covering (al-Gashiya), Falling (al-Waqiya), Imminent (al-Haqqa).

Encourage the children to do deeds of obedience to Allah and stock up additional blessings in preparation for the Day of Resurrection.

Explain to the children that the grave is the first stage of the Last Life.

Explain to them that three questions will be asked to the servant of Allah in the grave: "Who is your Lord? What is your religion? Who is your Prophet? Whoever answers these questions correctly will receive bliss as a reward, and whoever fails to answer them will be subjected to a painful punishment in the grave.

Point out to the children the Greatness of Allah and His Power, because He will bring out people from their graves for calculation (of their good and bad actions) and retribution.

Tell the children about some of the horrors of the Day of Resurrection: the proximity of the sun to the creatures, the scattering of scrolls with deeds, receiving an order for some to take a record with their deeds in their right hand, and for others in their left hand, passing through the Bridge over Hell (*sirat*).

Arouse in the children the desire to go to Paradise by mentioning some of its blessings, as well as about the reasons that lead to getting into Paradise. Arouse in the children the fear of going to Hell by mentioning some of the punishments in it, as well as the reasons that lead to going to Hell.

Encourage the children to pray to Allah for Paradise and gain entry to it through words and deeds, and with the mercy of Allah. Also encourage the children to turn to Allah for protection from Hell.

Read to the children of Surah at-Takwir (Surah 81), Al-Infitar (Surah 82) and "al-Inshikaq" (Surah 84) and relate their content to the topic studied in this lesson.

Purpose of this lesson:

- Explain to the children the meaning of the words "faith in the Day of Judgment".

- Tell the children about some of the events that will happen on the Day of Judgment.

- Explain to the children the Sharia judgment about the one who denies the Day of Judgment.

LESSON 32

BELIEVE IN PREDETERMINATION, BOTH THE GOOD OF IT AND THE BAD

The words "belief in predestination, both the good of it and the bad" means:

A firm belief that everything that happens, whether good or bad, happens according to the predestination of Allah.

Sharia evidence for belief in predestination is contained in the following Words of the Almighty:

"Verily, We created everything according to predestination" (Surah al-Qamar, verse 49).

Shariah judgment about who denies predestination: Such a person is a disbeliever in Allah Almighty!

TOPIC FOR DISCUSSION

What is the meaning of the words "belief in predestination, both good and bad"?

Give Sharia evidence for belief in predestination.

Whoever denies at least one of the six pillars of iman is ....

When misfortune befalls me, I say:

"Indeed, we belong to Allah, and to Him we will return! O Allah, reward me for my misfortune and give me something better in return!

NOTES FOR THE PARENT AND TEACHER:

Explain to the children the obligation to surrender to the will of Allah in His predestination, since the Prophet, peace and blessings of Allaah be upon him, said: "Allah predetermined destinies fifty thousand years before the creation of heaven and earth" (this hadith was transmitted by at-Tirmidhi, no. 2156).

Explain to the children that patience is needed when a person suffers misfortune or grief, for example, the death of a loved one, loss of property, illness of any organ of the body, etc...

Explain to the children that patience is the reason for receiving rewards from Allah, as the Messenger of Allah, peace and blessings of Allah be upon him, said: "Any Muslim who is pricked by a thorn or something worse than this, Allah surely forgives his bad deeds for this, and he is freed from his sins like a tree is freed from its leaves" (this hadith was transmitted by al-Bukhari No. 5648 and Muslim No. 2571).

Encourage the children to thank Allah and explain to them that this (thanking and being grateful to Allah) is the reason for the increase of His favors (blessings), as the Almighty said: "If you are grateful, then I will give you even more" (Surah "Ibrahim", ayat 7).

Purpose of this lesson:

- Explain to the children the meaning of the words "faith in predestination".

- Explain to the children the Sharia judgment about who denies predestination.

- Give the children the reference from the Quran or Authentic Hadeeth that Allah has created everything that exists with predestination.

LESSON 33

The third stage - IHSAN

(Islam) (Iman) (Ihsan)

The meaning of the word "Ihsan" is that:

You worship Allah as if you see Him, and if you do not see Him, then, indeed, He sees you.

Ihsan - the highest level of religion

Reference from the Quran or Authentic Hadeeth for ihsan are the following Words of Allah Almighty:

"Indeed, Allah is with those who fear God and who do ihsan (muhsinun)" (Surah an-Nahl, ayat 128).

TOPIC FOR DISCUSSION

Religion has three levels. Which one is the highest?

Define the word "ihsan" and give Sharia evidence for ihsan.

I am Muslim. I know that Allah hears and sees me, so I do not disobey Him by listening to or looking at what causes His Wrath!

NOTES FOR THE PARENT AND TEACHER:

Explain to the children that ihsan is perfection in worship both outwardly and inwardly, and ihsan is the highest degree of sincerity.

Tell the children some stories that point to ihsan. For example, the story of Umar ibn al-Khattab, may Allah be pleased with him, who once wanted to test a shepherd, telling him: "Sell me a sheep!" Then the shepherd answered: "I am a slave." Umar said: "And you tell your master that the wolf ate her." To which the shepherd replied: "But Allah does not deceive!" Then Umar, may Allah be pleased with him, wept, redeemed this shepherd from slavery and freed him, saying to him: "In this world, this word redeemed you from slavery, and I hope that it will free you in the last life!". Read more about this story in the book "Siyar alam an-nubala" ("Lives of wonderful people") by Imam al-Dhahabi, may Allah have mercy on him.

A person can achieve the degree of ihsan only if he is Muslim (Muslim) and believer (Mu'min).

Help to develop in the souls of the children the desire for performing rites of worship based on sincerity.

Purpose of this lesson:

- Explain to the children the meaning of the word "Ihsan".

- Give the children Sharia evidence for ihsan.

- Encourage the children to sincerely perform the rites of worship.

And in conclusion, praise be to Allah - the Lord of the worlds!

Peace and blessings be upon our Prophet Muhammad, his family members and all his companions!